SOLOS FOR THE CHANGING MALE VOICE

Edited, Arranged, and Composed by
Dave and Jean Perry

SHAWNEE PRESS
Vocal Library

Shawnee Press

EXCLUSIVELY DISTRIBUTED BY

HAL•LEONARD®
CORPORATION

7777 W. BLUEMOUND RD. P.O. BOX 13819 MILWAUKEE, WI 53213

Visit Shawnee Press Online at
www.shawneepress.com

Visit Hal Leonard Online at
www.halleonard.com

CONTENTS

Greenland Fishery **4**
> *An English sailing song that describes the efforts of an eighteenth century
> captain and his crew on their whaling expeditions into the icy waters
> of Greenland's coast.*

A Red, Red Rose **9**
> *A setting of Robert Burns's famous poem.*

John Henry **14**
> *John Henry tells of the legendary folk hero who worked laying rails
> for the railroads in the 1800s.*

Ezek'el Saw the Wheel **18**
> *The traditional spiritual based on the vision which the prophet,
> Ezekiel, had of a whirlwind.*

Jenny Kissed Me! **24**
> *The poem by James Henry Leigh Hunt was written in 1838 under the
> title, "Rondeau." Hunt was an editor of several periodicals in England,
> as well as a friend and promoter of Keats.*

The Coasts of High Barbary **27**
> *A Somerset chanty that tells of a battle between the English and
> a ship of Barbary pirates off the northern coast of Africa.*

Passing By **33**
> *This early seventeenth century anonymous poem has become part of the
> standard repertoire for the young singer. Edward Purcell's setting has
> been altered to accommodate the limited range of the changing voice.*

Pat-a-Pan **36**
> *A traditional Burgundian carol with original text from the eighteenth century,
> by Bernard de la Monnoye.*

GREENLAND FISHERY

Traditional English
Arranged by
DAVE *and* JEAN PERRY (ASCAP)

'Twas eigh-teen hun-dred and six-ty-one, on _ March the eigh-teenth _ day, We _ hoist-ed our col-ors to the top _ of the mast, and from Eng-land bore _ a-

way, and from Eng - land bore a - way. Our cap - tain stood on the

quar - ter - deck, with a spy - glass in his hand, "It's a

whale, and a whale, and a whale," cried he, "where she blows at ev - 'ry

span, brave boys, where she blows at ev - 'ry span."

Then the boats were launched and the men on board, with the whale-fish well in view. And well pre-pared were our jol-ly ship-mates to strike where the whale-fish blew, brave boys; To strike where the whale-fish blew. Then the whale was struck and the line played out, but he

38
gave such a flour-ish with his tail, he ___ cap - sized the boat ___ and we

41
lost ___ five ___ men, and we nev - er did catch ___ that ___ whale. And we

44
nev-er did catch ___ that whale.

48
"Hoist up the an - chor," our cap - tain cried, "Let us

leave this cold _ coun - try, where the storm and the snow _ and the

whale - fish do blow, and the day - light's sel - dom _ seen, brave boys, and the

day - light's sel - dom seen. And the day - light's sel - dom seen."

A RED, RED ROSE

Words by
ROBERT BURNS (1759-1796)

Music by
DAVE *and* **JEAN PERRY (ASCAP)**

IA0086

* No breath.

I will love thee still, my dear, While the sands of life shall

run. And I will love thee still, my dear,

While the sands of life shall run.

JOHN HENRY

Traditional Folk Song
Arranged by
DAVE *and* JEAN PERRY (ASCAP)

With a rhythmic "2" pulse (♩ = ca. 138)

This ol' ham-mer _____ killed John Hen-ry! _____

_____ This ol' ham-mer _____ killed John Hen-ry! _____

This ol' ham-mer _____ killed John Hen-ry. _____

But this ol' ham - mer _____ won't kill me. _____ This ol'

ham-mer _____ shines like sil - ver! _____ This ol'

EZEK'EL SAW THE WHEEL

Traditional Spiritual
Arranged by
DAVE *and* JEAN PERRY (ASCAP)

IA0086

air. The big wheel moved by faith. The lit-tle wheel moved by the

grace of God. A wheel in a wheel; _____ 'way in the mid-dle of the

air. Just let me tell you what a hyp-o-crite will do,

'way in the mid-dle of the air. He'll talk a-bout me and he'll

grace of God. A wheel in a wheel; _____ 'way in the mid-dle of the air.

Watch out, my sis - ter, how you walk on the cross,

'way in the mid-dle of the air. Your foot might slip and your

soul get lost! 'Way in the mid-dle of the air.

JENNY KISSED ME!

Words by
J.H. LEIGH HUNT (1784-1859)

Music by
DAVE *and* JEAN PERRY (ASCAP)

IA0086

* No breath.

THE COASTS OF HIGH BARBARY

Somerset Chantey
Arranged by
DAVE *and* JEAN PERRY (ASCAP)

til at last our frig – ate shot the pi – rate's mast a – way. A –

sail – ing down a – long the coasts of High Bar – ba – ry._____

"For

quar – ter! For quar – ter!" the sau – cy pi – rate cried. Blow

PASSING BY

Edward Purcell (1689-1740)
Arranged by
DAVE *and* JEAN PERRY (ASCAP)

Anonymous (17th Century)

IA0086

34

yet I love her till I die.

Her ges-tures, mo-tions and her smile, Her

wit, her voice my heart __ be-guile, Be - guile __ my heart, I

know not why, And yet I love her till I die.

IA0086

PAT-A-PAN

Words by
BERNARD DE LA MONNOYE (1641-1728)

Burgundian Carol
Arranged by
DAVE *and* JEAN PERRY (ASCAP)

Lightly (♩ = ca. 80)

Wil - lie, bring your lit - tle drum; Rob - in, bring your
* *Guil - lo, pran ton tam - bo - rin, Toi pran tai fleu -*

flute and come. When we hear the tune you play,
te, Ro - bin; Au son de ces in - stru - man, Tu - re - lu - re

* Pronunciation guide on page 39.

lu, pat - a - pat - a - pan. On this joy - ful win - ter day, let us sing and

dance and play.

Pronunciation Guide

Guillo, pran ton tamborin,
Gyee-yoh, prah taw tah-boo-reh,

Toi pran tai fleute, Robin;
Twah prah tay fleh-tuh, Raw-beh;

Au son de ces instruman,
Oh saw duh say eh-stree-mah,

Tu-re-lu-re-lu, pat-a-pat-a-pan;
Too-ruh-loo-ruh-loo, paht-ah-paht-ah-pah;

Au son de ces instruman,
Oh saw duh say eh-stree-mah,

Je diron Noei gaiman.
Zhuh dee-roh Noh-ehee gay-mah.